KILLING TREES AND WASTING INK

Poems & Prayers

DOUG GEISENDORFER

PROMINENT
BOOKS

5830 E 2nd St, Ste 7000 #9983
Casper, WY 82609
USA

Dedication

I started writing poems one day out of the blue,
Kind of like a fluke, just something to do!

I can't explain words, they bring me to life,
Like the spirit, my parents, my kids, and my wife.

So I dedicate this book to the Lord above,
The gift of life, and the family I love.

~ Doug

WARNING

This book was written by
A DUMB, BIG EARED, GOD FEARING
ELLITERATE COUNTRY BOY!

Content may not be well punctuated or spelled
correctly but is suitable for anyone who can read!

Contents

Killing Trees & Wasting Ink

When I'm writing a poem,
My brain is a tangled mess.
It just rattles on and on,
Like listening to an auctioneer I guess.

It always starts out simple,
And then it tries to grow.
It eventually ends up somewhere,
It seems I never know!

As I juggle words,
There's a message I'm trying to send.
If I juggle long enough,
I'll eventually find the end.

Some might make you happy,
And some might make you sad.
Some are pretty good,
And some are fairly bad.

But I hope you like my book of poems,
And all the crazy thoughts that I think.
Because otherwise, you wasted your money,
And I'm just killing trees and wasting ink!

Possum Holler

Up in the Northern Missouri hills,
There's a place called Possum Holler.
It don't take much to live around here,
We ain't got much need for a dollar.

Mama is a headed to the hen house,
With a butcher knife in bare feet.
I reckon she must be gonna shuck out a chicken,
An' fix us up somethin' to eat.

Daddy is a settin' in the shade,
A sippin' whiskey 'bout as fast as he can swaller.
Ol' Blue is a lyin' on the porch,
A scratchin' at the fleas underneath his collar.

JimBob is a pickin' at a banjo,
CindyLou is a dancin' a jig,
Grandad is a standin' out behind the barn,
Spittin' tobacca a yellin' woo—pig.

Granny lost her marbles
'Bout four years ago or maybe five.
She says she got abducted by Aliens,
An' Elvis is still alive.

Possum Holler ~

Aunt Louise is a wanderin' 'round the yard,
A tryin' to find our Apple Tree.
I bet if she would clean those Coke-bottle glasses,
The future she could probably see.

Uncle Henry lost his girlfriend
To some guy named Jimmy Black.
But Ol' Jimmy got struck by lightnin' last week,
So Uncle Henry got 'er back.

I'm just setting' here enjoyin' the day,
A tryin' to soak it all in,
An' as long as the good Lord is willin',
I'll get up tomorrow an' do it all over again.

We could move uptown with those big city folk,
In that rat race chasin' a dollar.
But I think life seems pretty dang good,
Right here in Possum Holler.

Wild Mustang

I was just a little boy
The day my daddy died.
He got bucked off and trampled
By a wild mustang he was trying to ride.

I remember feeling empty and scared
As Daddy laid there on the ground.
Screaming sirens and my momma crying
Was the only sound.

I made a vow right then and there,
My daddy's revenge I would get.
I'd hunt down every wild mustang there was
And break them all before I'd quit.

Well, I'm quite a bit bigger now
And my daddy is still in my heart.
I remember that solemn vow I made,
And I figured it's about time to start.

So I caught a ride to town one day
With my momma to pick up some stuff.
Lo and behold, I saw a wild mustang and yelled,
"Back up, it's about to get rough!"

I jumped up on that mustang's back
And got me a hand full of mane.
As I kicked and whipped and spurred that
    mustang,
Everybody looked at me like I was insane.
Well, he just stood there with his head down

Like he was scared or maybe just dumb.
So I kicked and whipped and spurred him some
    more
And said, "Paybacks are hell where I come from."

Right there in front of K-Mart,
Everybody started laughing like it was funny.
Then some old man walked up, put a quarter in
    my hand, and said,
"Cowboy, if you want to ride that mustang,
    you're gonna have to put in some money."

Beautiful Child

What a beautiful child
That God has given me,
What a wonderful person
He left me to oversee.

I'm excited, thankful, and scared
All at the same time.
Who this person ends up to be,
The responsibility is mine.

I have the love and knowledge,
My patience will be put to the test.
I'll try to be the best parent I can be,
And time will tell the rest.

As the years go by, I see so many changes
As I watch this child grow.
What's going to happen next?
I guess there's no way to know.

Sometimes it's frustrating,
You have to hold back your temper.
That can be fairly tough.
Sometimes they're sweet and innocent,
And you can't hug and kiss them enough.

We've had our ups and downs,
Somehow we've made it through.
When you're a parent, you can never give up
No matter what you do.

Every day I thank God for giving me this child
To raise and oversee,
But to tell you the truth, I think he gave me a child
To try to finish raising me!

My Little Hunter

My little Hunter
Wants to be just like me.
He is ambitious and excited
As he can possibly be.

When I used to go hunting,
I would go all alone,
But my little Hunter's big enough now
I can't leave him at home.

I've always been successful
Year, after year, after year,
But since I started taking my little Hunter,
I haven't got a single deer.

Spending time with my little Hunter
Is something I truly enjoy.
I just don't know how my dad went hunting,
Dragging along a little boy.

I'd leave him at home with his mama if I had my
        choice,
Because my little Hunter doesn't know how to
        whisper.
He uses his outside voice.

When my little Hunter walks through the timber,
He won't pick up his feet.
He's got pockets stuffed full of snacks;
All he wants to do is eat.

Question after question,
My little Hunter won't be quiet.
I beg him to sit still.
Please son, just try it.

My little Hunter says "I want to go home Dad.
I'm getting cold."
So I tell him some stories
That his grandpa told.

All the times he took me hunting,
All the time together we spent,
I'm doing everything I can
To keep my little Hunter content.

He says "We're not gonna see nothing Dad.
It's time for us to go."
As I think back, my little Hunter reminds me
Of a boy my dad used to know.

I start to laugh because it's frustrating to the point
Where it almost makes me mad.
I will have to say if my little Hunter keeps it up,
He is going to end up just like his dad.

Love at First Sight

The first time I saw her
Was at the Farm and Home store.
I will love you forever,
I stood there and swore.

She was the most beautiful thing
I ever had seen.
She was fine, fit, and equipped;
She was every man's dream.

I said I'll take you home,
I'll treat you just right,
I'll take special care of you,
And I'll kiss you each night.

Well, the first few years
Went along pretty good,
And I held to my word
The best that I could.

But the new wore off
And the lust all went.
She started to nickel and dime me.
Man the money I've spent!

Then all of a sudden,
things got really bad,
And I started to remember
All the others I've had.

I really hate to do it,
Especially since I swore,
But today I'm gonna go trade her in,
For another brand new lawn mower.

First Time

It was her first time
And my first time too.
It seemed neither one of us
Knew exactly what to do.

She was real nervous,
But I couldn't wait.
I knew with a little cooperation,
The result was going to be great.

I said Honey I've never done this before,
But I'll sure try my best.
I said you just hold real still
And let me do the rest.

So I put my hand on her butt
And sat on a stool.
As I rubbed and caressed her,
She looked at me like I was a fool.

I started rubbing her bosom
And it was soft to my touch.
She was wiggling around
Like she didn't like it that much.

So I just rubbed her real gentle
And talked to her real sweet,
I was hoping and praying
My satisfaction she would meet.

She finally gave in
And let me have my way.
It felt so good,
I told her we can do this every day.

Well, I have kept her around
For about eleven years now,
And every single day,
I still milk that old cow.

The Ride

We were told to leave her alone.
To tell the truth, we honestly tried.
But we were wanting to have some fun,
And we already broke everything else we had
      to ride.

If we could find an ounce of mischief,
Just go ahead and make it a double.
No matter what we did,
We always ended up in trouble.

So we got her up and brought her around.
There wasn't anyone in sight.
Take your time, let's think this over,
Make sure that everything's just right.

She wasn't very wide,
But she was long and pretty to the sight.
We'd never ridden anything like her before.
Grit your teeth and hold on tight!

I guess I'm ready if you are.
Go ahead and let her go.
This is the fastest thing I've ever been on.
She will flat get up and go!

The rush, the adrenaline, it's hard to explain,
On the verge of being out of control.
When it was finally over,
I took a deep breath as she came to a whoa.

I would like to race the neighbor kids.
I know we would surely win.
But we got to go put her up right now.
Maybe tomorrow we can do it again!

We had better keep our mouths shut
No matter what we do,
Because Dad is going to kill us if he finds out
We were sled riding in his canoe!

Living a Dream

My banker called me and said
Your payments are late.
If you could come in today,
That would be great.

So I chucked a little bit
Like I thought it was funny,
Because both of us know
I ain't got any money.

But I didn't hesitate.
I said I'd be right there,
Because my banker has never been
Nothing but fair.

He said how have you been doing?
Is everything going like it should?
I said no, as a matter of fact,
Things ain't really that good.

I said the cow won't milk,
And the chickens won't lay,
My tractor caught on fire
While I was baling hay.

The barn fell in
And my truck broke down.
I had to ride a horse
Just to get to town.

He said don't worry about it son,
Just sign another note.
There's a lot of other people
In the same darn boat.

Just keep your chin up.
We'll get you operating again.
Don't ever give up.
You'll eventually win.

If we extend your note another 10 years,
It can't do no harm.
It's just what you have to do
When you're living on a farm.

As I rode that horse home, I was thinking
Things must not be as bad as they seem.
I finally understand what my dad meant
When he said we're living a dream.

Thief

You are not really welcome,
But since you are here,
Go on in the kitchen
And get yourself a beer.

Don't worry about the door,
I'll fix it tomorrow again.
It never really did work right
From the last thief that kicked it in.

Go ahead and rummage around,
You have all night,
But everything of value
Is locked up in the safe real tight.

You can trash my place
And tear up all my stuff;
Knock yourself out
Until you think you've had enough.

You know you are just a low-life thief,
And there's nothing you can steal I can't replace,
But cheer up, since you're on camera,
You may as well have a smile on your face.

Poem About Nothing

I want to write a poem,
With a lot of truth, meaning, and heart.
The only problem is,
That I don't know where to start.

Should I write about love or life,
Is it good or is it bad?
Does it have truth and meaning,
Is it happy or is it sad?

It seems I'm always happy
Except for when I'm sad,
And things are always good
Except for when they are bad.

I never shed a tear
Except for when I cry,
And I always tell the truth
Except for when I lie.

I never laugh
Except for when something is funny,
And I'm never broke
Except for when I'm out of money.

It seems I'm always warm
Except for when I'm cold,
And I always follow orders
Except for when I don't do what I'm told.

I always work hard
Except for when I feel lazy,
And I always act mature,
Except for when I feel crazy.

I'm never pissed off
Except for when I'm mad,
And I'm never ever ecstatic
Except for when I'm glad.

I'm hardly ever hungry
Except for when I don't eat,
And I always play fair
Except for when I cheat.

I always hit my target
Except for when I miss,
But wait just a minute—
Where was I going with this?

I wanted to write a poem
With a lot of truth, meaning, and heart,
But this poem has been about nothing,
Right from the very start.

Resumé

I'm sending you this resumé
To see where it leads.
I'm anxious to find a career
That will completely suit my needs.

After you read this resumé,
I'm sure you will be satisfied.
I spent eight years in college,
So I know I'm more than qualified.

I guess I'll start out
And tell you a little more about me.
You're going to be impressed,
And I know you will plainly see.

My work ethic is outstanding,
And my attitude is great,
But I will not work a Saturday,
And every Monday I'll be late.

The first job I had I was a sanitary engineer,
But they just wanted me to pick up trash.
I quit because I had to wear gloves every day;
My hands broke out with a rash.

So then I got a job as a pillow tester,
But I couldn't stay awake.
So they moved me up to the mattress line,
But I quit because I only got one 30-minute break.

So then I got a job as a bank teller.
Dressing up made me feel kind of strange,
But after the second day, I got fired
Because I didn't know how to make change.

So I got a job as a chef at McDonald's.
I prepared all the food in the back,
But they let me go because they wouldn't
        understand
French fries taste better when they're black.

Now that you know my work history,
I guess you plainly see,
There's not a whole lot of people out there
With as much experience as me.

I'm excited and willing and ready to go to work.
I will be an asset to your company you can bet.
But I have sent out five other resumés to you,
And I haven't gotten a single call from you yet.

When I wrote the poem, "Tombstone," my four children were fairly small. One day shortly after my dad passed away, I was thinking. What would happen if I died today or tomorrow or before my kids were grown? What would happen if I wasn't here to give them guidance like my dad always tried to do for me? How do I know that they would know what I know? How do I know they would believe like I believe? So as I sat there and thought about it, I came up with a plan. I would write a poem to put on my tombstone so that throughout their lives, if they visit my stone, they would read my message. Then I realized that not just my kids would read this, and maybe I could help anyone who stumbled across my tombstone—right down to the person mowing the grass, if they would stop the lawn mower long enough to read this. Maybe I could make them stop and think because if you believe in Christ, death is not the end, it's the beginning.

Tombstone

I'm glad that you came,
But I'm not really here.
Don't be disappointed friend
And have no fear.

Don't get upset
And don't you cry,
Because now I have wings
And I know how to fly.

In the cold hard ground
My body may lay,
But I will see you again
On a much better day.

I will always be with you,
We are never apart.
I'm in your thoughts, I'm in your memory,
I'm in your soul, and I'm in your heart.

But right now I'm in the hands of my savior,
And he's not letting go.
He held to his word,
I just want you to know.

My sins were forgiven,
Into eternity I was enrolled.
Now I spend every day
Walking on solid streets of gold.

But I didn't get to Heaven
From all I achieved,
The only reason I'm here,
Is because I simply believed.

Christmas Day

On Christmas morning as you look
At all the gifts and presents under your tree,
Stare at the star for a little bit,
And remember how it came to be.

Both shepherds and wise men,
Came from near and far.
They were guided to Bethlehem,
By that wonderful star.

When you eat Christmas dinner,
And everyone gathers around the table,
Think about a cold and hungry infant,
In a manger in a stable.

Surrounded by cows,
Donkeys, goats, and sheep.
A newborn King lying there shivering,
Trying to sleep.

After dinner is over and your belly is full,
You're going to feel like taking a nap,
But instead, if there's a child in the house,
Tell them to jump up on your lap.

Tell them the story of a savior,
Sent from the heavens above.
Tell them about a person who's full of grace,
Compassion, mercy, and love.

He was put on earth to free us from sin,
And that was the only reason for him to live.
Eternal life is the greatest gift,
Anyone has ever give.

I wish you and your family the very best
This year on Christmas Day.
Be sure to thank our Lord and Savior,
Jesus Christ, in his name we pray.

Blessed

Blessed are the people
Who are generous and kind,
Blessed are the people
Who keep others on their mind.

Blessed are the people
Who are honest and sincere,
Blessed are the people
Who love without fear.

Blessed are the people
Who keep reality in sight,
Blessed are the people
Who know wrong from right.

Blessed are the people
Who are humble and proud,
Blessed are the people
Who shout it out loud.

Blessed are the people
Who keep Jesus in the future they see,
Blessed are the Christians,
Like you and me.

Daily Prayer

When the light of day fades away,
I bow my head and begin to pray.

As I search for the words I need to say,
I beg you Lord keep my sins at bay.

I know the debt you had to pay,
And I haven't exactly followed the path you lay.

As I stumbled through these days of gray,
In this game of life that I play.

As I contently try to find my way,
I know this sin is not to stay.

Please be with me every day,
Let me not be led astray.

Until the day I pass away,
From the book of life, my name you'll say.

Every night and every day,
I'm at your mercy, in your name I pray.

Spring Morning

It's a quiet spring morning,
There's not a lot going on,
As I sit and relax
In a chair on my lawn.

I noticed the ants are all working,
I watch as they gain.
I wish they could talk,
I bet they would never complain.

Suddenly a hummingbird
Catches my eye.
He checks every flower,
Man they can fly.

I watch as a robin
Rebuilds her nest,
Twig by twig,
She gives it her best.

The wrens have been gone
All winter long,
I sit and listen
As they sing me a song.

A woodpecker starts pecking,
He's throwing a fit.
He's making a racket,
I wish he would quit.

It's a busy spring morning,
There's a lot going on,
As I sit and relax
In a chair on my lawn.

Who Is Mother Nature?

Who is Mother Nature?
It seems nobody knows,
But the knowledge she gives us
Just grows and grows.

She's as strong as a hedge tree
That stands in a row.
She's as harsh as a winter
With six feet of snow.

She's fragile as a fetus
That grows in a womb.
She's beautiful as a flower
That's fully in bloom.

She shines like the snow geese
In a flock as they fly.
She's the reason an eagle
Builds their nest up so high.

She's the reason the antlers
Grow on a whitetail deer.
She's the reason the catfish swim
Up river to spawn each year.

She's the reason a butterfly
Survives in a storm.
She's the reason a hornets' next
Keeps it's perfect form.

She's the reason a groundhog
Burrows in so deep.
She's the reason a bear
Spends the winter asleep.

She's the reason a bobcat
Is so timid and shy.
She's the reason the fireflies
Light up the sky.

She's the reason an owl
Is so loud when they call.
She's the reason we have Winter,
Spring, Summer, and Fall.

We can't live without her,
Like honey for a bee.
She gives us our life.
She's the fruit on our tree.

How can someone so wonderful
Be so hard to see?
I'm really not sure,
But I think she wrote this with me.

The Trapper

I am a Trapper
And everyone knows,
From the top of my head
To the tips of my toes.

All summer long
I polish my gear,
And dream of the critters
I will catch this year.

A week before season
I get all uptight,
I'm nervous and restless;
I can't sleep at night.

I envision my trapline,
The money I'll make,
Not thinking of all
The abuse I will take.

From frostbitten fingers
To sore frozen feet,
I will stay out all day
With nothing to eat.

I will wade every river,
Every creek, every stream.
I will climb every mountain,
Chasing my dream.

By the end of the season,
All the fun that I had,
I don't remember last year
Hurting this bad.

I caught a lot of fur,
And I made a lot of cash,
But I spent most of it
On bait, beer, and gas.

You can laugh if you want,
But this ain't a joke,
Because now the season is over,
And I'm still flat broke!

Tips for Deer Hunting

If you want to be the best deer hunter
You can possibly be,
Then take a few tips
From a professional like me.

I've been a professional deer hunter
My entire life.
If you don't believe me,
You can just ask my wife.

It doesn't really matter how big of a gun
Or how fast of a bow,
It's not important what you're packing,
It's how much you know.

Ladder stands and climbing stands—
They say they're safe and sound,
But professionals like me
Feel safer on the ground.

They say the higher up you are
The more that you can see,
But what's gonna happen
If you got to go pee?

Trust me! Never plop down
By a tree covered with thorns.
Be sure and wear thick gloves
So you don't bust your knuckles with rattling horns.

Wear four pair of socks
So your toes don't get froze.
If you spill doe urine on your finger,
Never pick your nose!

Just sit still and be patient
On the ground or in a chair.
There's got to be a dumb one
Somewhere out there.

But don't sweat it! If you haven't got a buck yet
And the season is over and gone,
You can always buy a big buck
On Amazon!

Boondocker

Most kids have idols
That play football, basketball, baseball, or soccer.
But when I was kid, I looked up to a man
They called the Boondocker.

He was the greatest outdoorsman
I ever did know.
I hung onto every word he said,
As I continued to grow.

He was sitting next to me calling,
When I shot my first tom.
I was nervous and shaking,
But he whispered, "Try to remain calm."

He said if you want a big buck,
Hunt morning and night,
And always remember,
He's only out of sight.

Well, he was there
When I got my first big buck.
I was proud as could be as we loaded it
In the Gray Angel, his truck.

There was nothing he couldn't fix,
Nothing he couldn't do,
And if he spoke a word,
You could bet that it was true.

He was a master mechanic.
He could pick a guitar and sing.
You could consider yourself mighty lucky,
If you have ever been tucked under
The Boondocker's wing.

I don't think I ever asked a question
That he didn't have an answer,
But at 43 years old, he lost his life
To pancreatic cancer.

If I could ever give him enough credit,
I would say this is barely a start.
Because my uncle David Brumbaugh,
    "Boondocker,"
Will always have a special place in my heart.

Happy Being Me

People always said I was different,
Kinda hard to know, standoffish, and weird.
I was like a Lone Wolf that never followed the pack.
I guess that's what they feared.

I always stood by myself,
When everyone else flocked together.
I guess maybe you could say
I'm just a bird of different feather.

I had a normal father
And I had a normal mother,
But I must have got a defective gene,
From one or the other.

I never fit in to the cliques or groups
Back when I was in school.
They must have thought I was an idiot
Or maybe some kind of fool.

I never needed attention,
And I never liked being in a crowd.
I would sneak off somewhere I could think,
In a place that wasn't so loud.

When I have problems, I don't get upset
And whine and bitch and moan.
I just disappear into the woods
And work them out on my own.

I never needed advice from anyone
Or a shoulder where I could cry.
If I need help, I just drop to my knees
And reach my hands for the sky.

Why I am the way I am
Must be hard for you to see.
The reason I'm so different,
Is because I'm just happy being me.

Ol' Buster

Back when I was a boy,
It's been 30 years or more,
There was an old denim rug
That laid just inside our back door.

When folks would stop by
To visit or eat,
They would walk right on in
And wipe the dirt off their feet.

When the old rug would get too dirty,
We would take it out the door,
Shake it out a bit,
And lay it right back on the floor.

One cold winter night,
When the snow was fairly deep,
I asked my mom if Ol' Buster
Could come in the house to sleep.

She said he's just an old hound dog,
And he stinks really bad.
With a disgusted look on her face,
She looked at my dad.

I knew my dad wouldn't have a whole lot to say,
You see,
Because he loved that old coondog
Just about as much as me.

I said Dad do you remember when
The coons and foxes used to get our chickens?
Since I got Ol' buster,
We ain't had a single one missin'.

Ol' Buster ~

Don't forget the time you lost your job
And was down on your luck.
Ol' Buster treed enough coons that winter
To make the payments on your truck.

Then there was that time our compass was stuck
And we got lost in the fog.
We would have spent all night trying to find the truck
If it wasn't for that old coondog.

My dad said I guess you're right.
He has earned his keep.
He does deserve a nice warm place
Where he can sleep.

He said just run on out
And get Ol' Buster, Doug.
He can sleep right there by the back door,
On that old denim rug.

Turkey Hunt

My alarm clock is buzzing,
I can hardly wait.
I've been preparing all year
For this very date.

The first day of Turkey Season
I will never miss,
So I lean over and give
My wife a goodbye kiss.

I said wish me luck
Be ready for a treat,
Because this year I'm gonna bring home
A nice tom turkey to eat.

She said you're wasting your time,
With a funny little grin.
I said Honey, there's no way that turkey
Is going to outsmart me again.

I've watched all the movies,
I know every trick,
And besides this year, my calls
Don't sound like a turkey that's sick.

I bought some new decoys
To stick in the ground.
I even bought a couple
That look like they are moving around.

I bought a new shotgun
That cost a lot of loot,
Not to mention the hundreds
I spent On this camouflage suit.

I have paint on my face,
I'm ready to go.
Just wait until I get home, Honey,
I'm gonna say I told you so.

Turkey Hunt ~

I wandered off into the darkness,
Trying not to make a sound,
When all of a sudden, I trip
And fall to the ground.

I dropped all my gear,
It made a kerthud.
Now my brand-new shotgun
Has a barrel full of mud.

I rummaged around
And found a long stick.
I have got to clean it out,
And I've got to do it quick!

It's starting to get daylight.
I'm going as fast as I can.
I will never live it down
If I show up empty-handed again.

I crossed a wire fence.
My brand new camouflage britches are torn.
When I got to my favorite hunting spot,
I sat on a Black Locust thorn.

I let out a yell,
And then started to cry,
As the sound of flying turkeys
Filled up the sky.

I yanked out the thorn,
Let me tell you it smarted,
Then suddenly I realized,
My hunt was over before it started.

As I walked back home
With my head hung in defeat,
I think it may be easier to go to the grocery
    store
And buy a nice Butterball to eat.

Conservation

When I was growing up, hunting, fishing, and
        trapping
Was the way I was taught to live,
But you can't just take from nature,
You have to learn to give.

If you take a little,
Give a little back,
And everything in nature
Will stay on track.

Plant food plots, create habitat;
There's a lot that you can do.
We need to take care of nature
So the next generation can enjoy it too.

I love the reward
And I love the taste,
And I always try not to let anything
Go to waste.

Every single creature,
Every single thing,
God made it for a reason,
No question should it bring.

From fish and bees
To animals and trees,
Step gently on nature
I beg you please.

Everything has a purpose;
Everything has a reason.
That's why things flourish,
Throughout every season.

I am a hunter, a fisherman, and a trapper,
But it's not a killing sensation.
I love everything that lives,
That's why I'm conservation.

Living Off the Land

Things have changed
So much over time,
Now if people want something to eat,
They stand in a welfare line.

I can't say that I blame them,
It's how they were taught to live.
Just keep your hand out,
Take all that they have to give.

I'm not making fun of anybody
For doing what they are able,
I just don't trust the government
To keep food on my table.

When I was growing up,
I was taught a different way,
So listen real close
To what I have to say.

If you're not the hunter,
Then you're the prey.
Feed somebody a meal,
They will live for a day.

If you teach them to hunt and fish,
They will eat for life.
All you need to survive
Is a gun, bow, or knife.

I don't want to offend anybody,
But I hope you understand.
You will never go hungry
If you're living off the land!

What You Leave Behind

They say it doesn't matter what you have,
It's what you leave behind.
Look at the history of this land,
It's crazy what you will find.

Columbus was shipping sugar,
And then he got lost.
The Native American way
Is what it eventually cost.

They lived on this land
For thousands of years,
Until we put those poor people
On a trail of tears.

We took the land away
They were willing to share;
We've raped it, abused it,
And trashed it without a care.

You might think what we've done
Is necessary, just, and sound,
But stop for a minute
And look around.

The water is no longer fit to drink,
The air is no longer clean;
Everywhere you look there is trash and landfills,
But they say we are going green.

When I see what's happening around me,
It fills my eyes with tears;
We have ruined this land
In just a little less than 250 years.

If you think I'm being irrational,
You'll have to forgive my haste;
We've turned this land into a place
Of chemicals, pollution, and hazardous waste.

If you can't see what we've done to this place,
Then I guess you must be blind;
Native Americans lived here for over twelve
        thousand years,
And artifacts are all they left behind.

My Prayer

Sweet Lord, my savior,
Please be with me,
A worthless sinner
I was born to be.

You are the only perfect person
To ever walk the Earth.
I can never live up
To all you are worth.

My cup runneth over
For so many years,
Yet I often find myself
Drowning in tears.

I know I have
Only myself to blame.
You are the only one
Who can rid me of shame.

I'm not worth all the pain and suffering
You had to endure,
So thank you Lord
That your love is so pure.

Thank you, Lord,
For your mercy and grace.
Please free me from sin,
Please don't leave a single trace.

Someday Lord

I've struggled through life,
And I've seen my share of hell.
I've committed my share of sins,
And I'm so ashamed I won't tell.

I've cheated and I've lied,
And all the Devil's ways I've tried to use.
I've took things that didn't belong to me,
And I've drank my weight in booze.

I've done some pretty awful stuff,
And other people took the blame.
Sometimes I'd like to crawl in a hole
And rot away in shame.

Although I know I've been blinded,
I'm trying to keep you in sight,
So that maybe someday Lord,
I might get something right.

I Am an Army

I am an army,
And I'm not afraid to fight.
I am an army,
And I know what's wrong and what's right.

I am an army,
The end is surely near.
I am an army,
Please don't have any fear.

I am an army,
I wish you'd follow me.
I am an army,
Can't you plainly see?

I am an army,
The word of God is on my mind.
I am an army,
And I don't want to leave you behind.

I am an army,
And I will proudly stand.
I am an army
Because I've got the world's most powerful weapon in my hand.

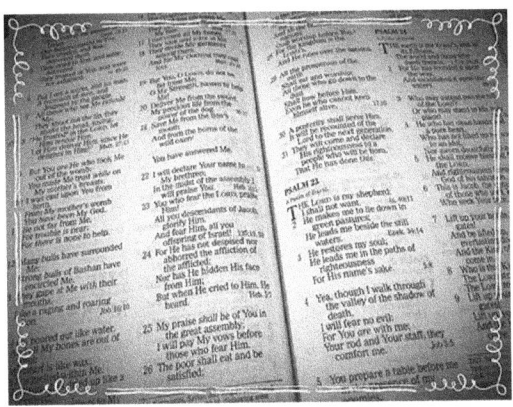

The Ones I Love the Most

I thank the ones
I love the most,
The Father, the Son,
And the Holy Ghost.

God who made me,
Jesus who saved me,
And the spirit and strength
The Holy Ghost gave me.

Without them I'm just
A worthless piece of flesh,
Like a fisherman without
His nets made of mesh.

Like a preacher
Without a Gospel to preach,
Like a teacher
Without curriculum to teach.

The ways of the Devil
I try to resist,
So that some day in Heaven
I might exist.

Lost on Earth,
I'll continue to roam,
Until the day
They bring me home.

Place I Want to Live

I read about a place I want to live,
Where I can find some peace.
It doesn't cost anything to live there;
You don't rent, buy, or lease.

A place where people are friendly
And there's people you can trust.
A place where everyone is honest
And religion is a must.

A place where wages are high
And the cost of living is low.
Truth and forgiveness
Is the only way they know.

A place where you never struggle,
The work has already been done.
A place you never have to fight,
The war has already been won.

A place where everywhere you look
There's a familiar face.
A place where there's lots of love,
Mercy, and grace.

A place that will never perish,
I can finally call my home.
Hopelessly lost,
I will no longer continue to roam.

Such a place
Sounds far-fetched as it can be,
But it's real, and it's already been prepared
For those who believe.

Decisions

You will have to make a lot of decisions
Throughout your life.
You can choose your occupation, your religion,
Your husband, or your wife.

Sometimes you can change your decisions,
At pretty much any time.
Sometimes you're stuck with your decisions,
Because you can't afford to lose what you might leave behind.

If you lose some things in life,
You'll never get them back.
It seems when I keep the faith,
My life stays right on track.

Do you ever worry
About the future and what it might bring?
Do you ever worry about life?
It's such a fragile thing.

If you lose the faith,
You'll lose the life.
It's like standing
On the edge of a knife.

Be careful which way you lean,
You just might slip and fall.
Because life is your decision
After all.

Crazy People

Do you know someone who's crazy,
Kinda weird, or not right?
Do they talk funny, or act strange,
Or are not so pretty to the sight?

Do they wear crazy clothes, drive a crazy little car,
Or paint their house a crazy color of paint?
Sometimes it's hard to figure out who's weird, who's not right,
Who's crazy, and who really ain't.

I try not to avoid crazy people,
Most of them won't hurt you, offend you, or try to cramp your style.
I think you would be entertained and surprised at what you might learn,
If you just sit and talk with them a while.

I have met some pretty crazy people,
Though their brains might need to be checked.
But the truth is I like crazy people,
At least you know exactly what to expect.

I'll Be Home When I Get Back

Honey, I'm going shed horn hunting again,
To try to find the other half of a big rack.
She said when will you be home?
I said I'll be home when I get back.

Honey, I'm going mushroom hunting.
I'm not quitting until I fill my sack.
She said when will you be home?
I said I'll be home when I get back.

Honey, I've only got two days to camp and
    turkey hunt.
My boss won't cut me no slack.
She said when will you be home?
I said I'll be home when I get back.

Honey, I'm going squirrel hunting,
See how many tree rats I can whack.
She said when will you be home?
I said I'll be home when I get back.

Honey, I will see you later.
There's a fishing hole I've been waiting to attack.
She said when will you be home?
I said I'll be home when I get back.

Honey, I'm headed to the field.
I've got some hay to bail and stack.
She said when will you be home?
I said I'll be home when I get back.

Honey, I've been deer hunting all day,
And I shot a big buck I need to track.
She said when will you be home?
I said I'll be home when I get back.

When I got home, there was a note on the table.
It said she's sick of me and has had all she can hack.
She said she's not sure where she's going,
And she's not sure if she's coming back.

I'm not sure what her problem is.
She must be smoking crack.
I always told her exactly where I was going
And exactly when I would be back.

Hickory Switch

When I was a boy growing up,
I was taught there are a lot of good uses for a hickory switch.
You could use them as a bank pole to catch
Flatheads and channel catfish.

You could use them to walk through the pasture
And knock down milk weeds and thistles.
My grandpa taught me how
To take one and make a hickory whistle.

It makes a really good handle
For a pitchfork, shovel, or an ax.
It also makes good firewood,
And it very seldom cracks.

I can make you a bow and some arrows
That will shoot as true as your heart would desire.
But I'll have to say I found out the hard way
That the best use for a hickory switch is to set a child's butt on fire!

Supply & Demand

My boss walked up to me the other day.
He said listen up son I've got a lot to say.

We've got to do our best to keep the upper hand.
This world is all about supply and demand.

He said we've got a lot that we need to get done.
I know working overtime ain't that much fun.

We're behind on orders and falling further behind.
You're the only help that we can find.

He said we need you son and we need you bad.
Just cancel those weekend plans that you had.

He said we've been working eight hour days,
but now we're going to ten.
Just hang in there son; we will get caught up again.

I smiled at him like I thought it was funny.
I said sounds good to me, just give me more money.

He said what do you mean more money?
I thought you would understand.
I said yes sir I do, but you're the one who started talking about
supply and demand.

Day by Day

Day by day,
I watch my life pass by.
As I see what's happening around me,
I wonder why I try.

Handouts and Welfare checks
Are all half of Americans have known.
Meanwhile I'm breaking my back
And working my fingers to the bone.

I take pride in being an American
And in loving my Neighbor,
As the upper class gets fat
Off of the fruits of my labor.

Our Government is corrupt
And crooked as can be.
I can't help but question
The fact that I'm free.

I'm tired of being overtaxed
And underpaid.
Is this the same Country
Our Forefathers made?
I will continue to work and struggle
Through life only by choice,
But it's time for the Working Class people
To stand up America.
We have a voice.

Fuzzy's Trucking

When you hear that jake break
Coming into town,
You can bet I'll be trucking
Until the sun goes down.

I haul grain, rock,
Dirt, or sand.
I'm the best in the business
I hope you understand.

You can count on me anytime,
I'll get the job done
Rain or shine.

No job too big,
No job too small.
All you gotta do
Is give me a call.

All your expectations
My business exceeds.
You can count on Fuzzy
For all your trucking needs!

Yuppie

I was headed to the field with my combine.
Some guy in a fancy little car was honking his horn and throwin' a fit.
He was trying to pass and flipping me off,
Being as obnoxious as he could get.

I pulled over and let him pass by.
I could tell he wasn't much of a charmer.
Then I thought, does that idiot know
That the cotton that made his fancy suit and tie came from a farmer?

Our corn, our soybeans, and wheat are in everything he eats,
Not to mention the fresh produce we supply.
His fine wine, his beer, and his whiskey
Come from our grapes, our hops, and our rye.

A couple miles later, he was flagging me down
To help with a flat tire on the side of the road.
I said I would really like to help you, but I'm busy feeding the world.
If I was you, I would just have it towed.

The Dance

The first thing you do
Is go around and around,
Three or four times
And then you spin her around.

You only go that way
Just one time,
Then you head through the middle
And spin her on a dime.

You go back and forth
And spin her around all day,
Or until you get done
Mowing down hay.

Green Beans

We plant green beans,
We hoe green beans,
We till green beans, and sweat.

We pull weeds out of green beans,
We pick green beans,
We snap green beans, and sweat.

We can green beans,
We freeze green beans,
All that we can get.

This winter when we're eating green beans,
We won't complain a bit, you can bet!

Signs

Some things in life
Are hard to see;
Other things in life
Are plain as can be.

Sometimes you're so full of life
It's hard to explain;
Sometimes you're empty
And feel nothing but pain.

Do you ever get sick of life
And feel there's no way out?
You're never going to find what you're looking for
Living in doubt.

Have you ever been looking for something in life
And searching everywhere,
Then suddenly you realize
It has always been there?

Sometimes in life you look too hard
For the things you're trying to find,
And all you really need to do
Is slow down and read the signs.

This beautiful mushroom is called chicken of the woods. It is orange and white, grows in the fall of the year, and really does taste like chicken.

Photos by Rick Whiles

Woodsman

I've been called a Redneck and a Hillbilly
And my daddy said I was his pride and joy.
I've been called an illiterate, dumb,
Back-woods, big-eared country boy.

When people talk about hunting, fishing, and trapping,
I sure draw a lot of attention.
When people talk about women and politics and the ways of the world,
Those things I'd rather not mention.

I can hunt down, trap, or track
Any type of creature.
I think like a wild animal and adapt to their environment;
The woods is my best teacher.

I can go to extremes
That most people can't meet.
I can find food
That most people wouldn't eat.

You can call me what you want,
But a woodsman would be fair,
Because a woodsman can adapt to anything
And live anywhere!

Poets and Preachers

Some make you laugh,
And some make you cry.
Some give you guidance,
And some leave you wondering why.

Some make you angry,
And some make you confused.
Some make you feel peaceful,
And some leave you feeling used.

Some speak fiction,
And some speak fact.
Some lead you astray,
And some keep you on track.

Some give you comfort,
And some give you pain.
Some are intelligent,
And some are insane.

They are both human,
And most mean well.
But you need to be careful.
There's a big difference between heaven and hell.

A poet can entertain you
And may lead you away from your goal.
A preacher can speak the truth to you
And may eventually save your soul.

They are two different characters
With two different features.
I will tell you the truth,
It's a whole lot easier to be a poet than it is to be a preacher!

The End

Now that you have reached the end,
I hope you like the writing I do.
I try to write from my heart,
About my life and things that are true.

I've put a lot of time and thought into this book.
For a guy like me, it was quite a task.
If I could get a favor from you,
Please do exactly as I ask.

Tell everybody you know about my book,
Share it, or give it out on a loan.
Maybe they'll like it too
And possibly buy their own!

About the Author

Doug Geisendorfer grew up on a small farm in northeast Missouri where he spent time working, running the wilderness, and going to church. In his spare time, he enjoys hunting, fishing, trapping, and writing poems and country/bluegrass songs. Doug and his wife are raising their four children on the family farm where he grew up. Many of these poems and stories have been inspired by true stories. May you enjoy them all!

www.ingramcontent.com/pod-product-compliance
Lightning Source LLC
Chambersburg PA
CBHW041125120626
46547CB00019B/2855